"Unauthorized Trump: How I Handed Hillary the Presidency" © 2016 by Kreston Kent

Published by
Keel Publications
P.O. Box 160155
Austin, TX 78716

All inquiries may be directed to:
info@krestonkent.com
www.krestonkent.com

Published July 2016

ISBN-13: 978-1535089746
ISBN-10: 1535089741

Unauthorized TRUMP
How I Handed Hillary the Presidency

My Confession of the Greatest Ruse Ever Perpetrated upon the American People — Unauthorized Donald TRUMP

by KRESTON KENT
*M.A. Government
University of Virginia*

Amazon & iTunes Category #1 Bestselling Author of *The Literary Genius of Lil Wayne*

From: Donny <thedonald@trump.com>
Subject: 2016
Date: June 07, 2008 at 10:35:58 PM EST
To: Hill <Hillary@clintonfoundation.org >

Hill

I've got a plan for 2016. Let's talk.

D

Donald J. Trump
President and CEO Trump Enterprises

Author's Preface

Upon the announcement of his Presidential bid, suspicions as to Trump's motives abounded: Self-aggrandizement? Ego indulgence? Business boost? Future reality TV efforts? My own immediate suspicion has become a popular one: Trump's purpose was to secure the Presidency for Hillary Clinton.

It's a suspicion that can't be un-thought. Once it takes hold of your mind, it frames every news cycle and every action by Candidate Trump: He must be deliberately pursuing a Clinton Presidency; there's no other explanation.

It is well known that Trump has been a contributor to the Clintons' campaigns and that his past positions leaned liberal and Democratic. Trump's business success has also risen under Democratic Presidents and has taken a hit in both major economic crises brought on by Republican policy regimes (1989 and 2008 – that's the economic crisis

of 1989, not the disastrous but wildly popular –
much like Trump's primary campaign – Taylor
Swift album).

Clinton has been beaten by an insurgent candidate
before, and she's a much weaker candidate now
eight years later. But she benefits from demographic
shifts that make a Democratic Presidency nearly
certain, barring major candidate flaws, but she has
enough of those to lose to a moderate Republican
with clean hands who could appeal to
Independents – a Jon Huntsman or a John Kasich.

That's where Trump steps in. He couldn't have
counted on winning the primary, but he knew he
could make it enough of a shitshow to doom the
GOP candidate. Without Trump, the 2012 GOP
Primary circus would not have repeated itself, at
least not to near the same extent; with Trump, it
became even more of one. Trump became Michele
Bachmann, Ron Paul, Newt Gingrich, Rick
Santorum and most importantly, Herman Cain, all
rolled into one. In so many ways, Cain's was a dry
run for a Trump sham-candidacy.

By ensuring the insolubility of the GOP going into 2016, Trump locked up a Clinton Presidency (all the more due to the symbiosis between Trump and Bernie Sanders). Trump could not have imagined that he'd actually win the GOP primary, and he didn't need to. All he had to do was set up the Republican candidate to fail. But Bernie Sanders came along and jumpstarted the cultural dynamic that sparked a reactionary response on the GOP side, catapulting Trump from a dead-end, flash-in-the-pan leader in the polls – a la Cain – to a leading vote-getter. While Trump held an early lead in the primary polls, without Sanders it likely would have bottomed out before the actual votes. But when Sanders catalyzed the voters' latent anti-establishment anger, Trump played the other side of the same coin. Imagine it: a GOP [albeit newly minted] billionaire New York mogul tapping into the populist socialist anti-Wall Street sentiment stoked by the America's most liberal Senator. On opposite sides of the political spectrum [personality-wise, not fully issue-wise], the two fed off each other in a "Bern"ing fire that ultimately consumed itself and left no one but

Hillary standing. Sanders' righteous indignation became indistinguishable (to the general public) from Trump's outlandishness, leaving the safe (but uneasy) choice, Hillary, coasting to the White House. When Trump actually found himself in a competitive position for the general election – leading some polls and with a foot in the door to mainstreaming himself – he slammed the door shut with a series of absurd stunts that cemented his November defeat. At that point, more and more voters and pundits caught on to his Great Ruse. In recent days and weeks, major news outlets including the Washington Post, New York Times and CNN have openly speculated about Trump's apparent "self-sabotage," "campaign malpractice" and "Trump hurting himself." They recognize that he's going out of his way to lose. He even teased the possibility of walking away from an imagined electoral victory without serving, further guaranteeing his own defeat.

This account imagines that Mr. Trump would not let his accomplishment – deliberately getting Hillary elected – be hidden from history, and that his account of the scheme would follow at some point after her inauguration.

Here are the unauthorized autobiographical words Trump might use to tell the story of the Greatest Ruse ever perpetrated upon the American people: a sham candidacy conducted to ensure an opponents' election to the Presidency of the United States.

Unauthorized

Mr. Trump's

Introduction

Only a true loser would let his greatest accomplishment fade into history. I've spent my life building an empire. We're talking Napoleonic, Stalinistic, Putinesca Empire. – Putinesque? No. What is that? "esque"? People say that? Sounds... How can I say this? Dandy. No. – Putinesca!

You know, Vladimir and I are good friends. I've been a great friend of the Russians since I've been in business. Great, great friend. Except Gorbachev: he was a loser. I like Putin. Let me tell you, Obama could learn a lot from Putin if he paid any attention to what was going on overseas. He's oblivious, or worse. (That's a joke, people. I don't really believe Barack has a secret agenda. Jesus, what do you take me for?)

How can I call Gorbachev a loser when I "lost to Hillary"? If anyone thinks I lost anything, think again. I did not lose this election. If I wanted to win, I would've won. I did win. We won. But it was my plan, so I won. I won in a way nobody's ever won before.

Look at everything that happened in the campaign: it went exactly the way I wanted. Exactly. Believe me. They said I couldn't win the primary. I wasn't even trying to win the primary, and I won anyway. If I'd won the Presidency, that would've been the failure. President would be a demotion for me. Big demotion. Just look at my hotel down the street from the White House. Who's doing better in life? You tell me.

What do they say "cockblocked"? I've been known to steal the show when it comes to taking a woman home. This time, I cockblocked the GOP and put a woman in office. The best thing? She wouldn't have needed my help, because the Republicans are so incompetent. So incompetent. They wouldn't have put up a real candidate anyway. But we had to guarantee it.

If you thought Mitt Romney was bad. And boy was

he bad! The biggest loser. The biggest. I wasn't even trying to get the nomination. That's how bad it is, people. Or that's how good I am. I beat eighteen of the top Republicans. Talk about losers. You can't beat a guy named Barak Hussein Obama? Are you kidding me? And this time was no different. They weren't running against Hillary. They were running against Barak. Three straight losses. They need to disband the whole party. Change the name. The brand is ruined.

Nobody has ever given America a slap in the face like I'm giving them. Whap! It's the biggest wake-up call. I can't let this stay secret. I can't die before I can share it with you. I'm writing it down in case something happens to me. You never know. I've never written anything in my life. You think I wrote those books? Why would I do that? Writing is artsy fartsy. I'll tell you: I had a cousin who studied creative writing. There's a lot more I could tell you about him, if you know what I mean. You think I'm going to sit down like a lady in front of a typewriter and write a book? You run a business like mine, you can't take the time to write a book. Why do something if you can pay someone to do it for you? What good is money if you can't pay people to do things for you? Some things, not all things. If you're a man at all – I don't care how much money you have – you never have to pay for *some things*, if you know what I mean. Never. Talk about losers.

If you're reading this before Hillary takes office, I've either been hacked bigtime or I'm looking down on you from that biggest Trump Tower in the sky.

Look. It's simple: I gave it to Hillary.

Don't believe it? Don't be a sucker. There are millions of suckers out there. Millions! I proved it. Don't be one of them. You think Trump University was a sham? How about Trump Candidacy?! Are you kidding me?

This is the problem with America today. Say what you will about me, I'm educated. That's the problem. You have no idea what's going on. There are so many, so many – I don't know the numbers but it's a lot! – who can't name which party the President is from. How can you vote like that? This is how I'm talking out of my ass and still getting more votes than any Republican in history. The American people don't have a clue. It's time for a wake-up call. I'm doing the greatest service to our country. I don't want to think about where the country would've gone if we hadn't done this. This is going to change things.

Think about it, it's really the greatest gift I could've given. It's a great gift. And you're gonna say, "oh! it's so horrible what he did." They'll say that for a day or two but then they'll realize. The country will be better off for it. Better to learn the lesson this way and learn it now, and that's all I did.

When people realize what I did, they're going to look in the mirror and stop being patsies. They're going to say to the mirror "what was I thinking?" Next time, they're gonna vote smarter. You can't vote for Trump and then go four years and do nothing about it after you found out what's really going on. How many of my voters are going to read up on politics and world affairs before the next go 'round? I'm the first to admit I don't know a lot about politics, and look what I did! I don't have time to stay current on foreign affairs. You can't be a Jack of All Trades and run a multi-billion dollar empire. You just can't do it.

My voters are basically Brexit voters, which is what I said (but they didn't have a clue). They have *no idea* what they're doing. They voted "no" first, and *then* searched "What is the E.U.?" Did you see this? They voted first, then searched for what they were voting after the fact. They had no idea what they were voting for. What's a vote for Trump *actually for*? I couldn't tell you.

Republicans have been doing this for years. We've all seen it: poor white southern voters reducing taxes for the wealthy! I love it. I pay no taxes. Nothing. Zero. Zilch. Thank you, Alabama!

But you know what? I don't need it. I'd be happy to pay taxes. I won't do it if I don't have to, but if I have to do it, legally, I'm happy to do it. I need a thriving economy way more than I need low taxes. I need real estate booms. The bust cycles? I know when to get out and how to get out. You've heard me say this: I know how to use the laws, I know how to cut deals, I know the lay of the land. Look at Atlantic City. Nobody cleaned up in Atlantic City like I did.

But it's not just the laws. This is where Hillary comes in. My old pals, Hill and Bill. Gotta love 'em. Two sides of the same coin. These people know how to get it done. Just like me. I love 'em. We go way back. Way back. It's a beautiful, beautiful thing.

Legislation, economic policy, blah blah blah, yap yap yap. Enough already. Shut up about it. You've heard it before: politics is personal. I gotta tell you something: business is more personal. To cut deals, you gotta grease wheels. I've been greasing the Clintons for decades. Decades. And boy are they loyal to me. Am I loyal to them? Am I ever! Together, we pulled off the greatest election deal in history.

They said I wasn't a real candidate because I was a reality TV star. You know who the real reality TV stars are? Hill and Bill. Not because they're on the news. They're in a drama! A miniseries, whatever you call it. They're Frank and Claire Underwood. Frank and Claire are the TV. Bill and Hill are *reality* TV. If you can't see how real that show is, I can't help you. I love the show; it's a great show.

The status quo could've gone on forever if not for –
excuse me – f%cking Barak Hussein Obama,
okay? This guy. This guy. He wasn't supposed to
win. He wasn't supposed to win. Let me tell you
how many deals I had to put off or renegotiate or
make concessions on the deals. My credibility was
shot for at least a year. I had things lined up for
Hillary to take the "reigns" in 2008. When Barak
won – and look, we're friends now; I built bridges, I
made peace offerings, and he plays the game like
the rest of them – but when he won, something had
to be done.

I still don't really like the Obamas. They're normal.
Average. Boring. They could do so much more, but
they're caught up in this idea of a loving family.
"Oooooo! We're such a loving family!" Get over it.
That's not how you build an empire. It's cute. It's
sweet. It's nice. It's not how you build an empire.
Yeah, he was President for eight years. He got
lucky. He ran against an incompetent party. It's the
most incompetent, non-competition in history. You
run Barak against any other party in history, he
loses. Hands down. It was luck. Hope? Puh-lease.

After that, the only way we were going to get Hillary in office was to take extraordinary steps, and I was the only one who could do it. Nobody has ever pulled this off. Nobody. Not anything like it, and frankly no one ever will again. I'm the only one – the only one – who could do this.

Think about it: millions. Tens of millions. Voting for me. I was trying to lose! Guaranteeing a loss. There were so many times when I could've won. Hill knows it. Bill knows it. I'm ten times the politician she will ever be. She's a policy nut. She's a nerd. But she has balls. And she's determined.

When I was deliberately trying to lose! I go out and do something that would drive any reasonable human being... What was it with the Grinch? 38-and-a-half feet? They wouldn't want to get within a radius of me. You saw it in Austria, you saw it in France. You saw it in Britain. The nutjobs can do well in elections. They may not win, but they come close. It's human nature. You get uneducated, and you get tribal. I blow a loud horn. I'm confident. I'm charismatic. People follow.

Wake up, America! Wake up.

I wasn't planning to win the nomination, but it made the job so much easier. It basically gave me complete control. Complete. I was just trying to hamstring the nominee, not be the nominee. When we came up with this plan, we didn't even consider the nomination. Didn't even consider it. But along came Bernie.

At one point, my kids even told me how I could win the general; not that I needed them to. They liked the idea. I had to explain how bad that would be. They liked it because then they could run things more.

You saw it. You saw how many times I was ahead in the polls and then shot myself in the foot. I couldn't drive the nutjobs away from me for very long. I had to keep at it.

Believe me, if I'd have wanted to win, I would've won. But why would I want to win? It's a shit salary – I wouldn't ever take a salary: I take profits – you can't do business while you're in office; you live in a shitbox and the city is built on a swamp. Now, don't get me wrong, there are many reasons to *visit* D.C. My new hotel down the block is one of them. It's beautiful. It's amazing. You don't want to stay anywhere else if you're going to D.C. Forget the St. Regis, okay? Stay at my hotel. It blows the St. Regis away, frankly. If I wanted the job, I would've taken the suite for four years and let Pence live in the White House.

And this is the lesson: America has gotten stupid. So stupid. That's it. America is stupid. The America I grew up in died a long time ago. The only thing that's the same is racism. When you have ignorance, you get racism. Fear of the unknown. It's obvious. If you don't know anything, you get afraid and angry. Racism isn't dead until ignorance is dead. It's far from dead. American is so stupid. If you don't know basic geography, you will hate foreigners, because you fear them. So here's what we had to do:

Republicans can't win right now. We knew that, they knew that. 2012 proved that. They had one chance to win 2012 and they didn't take it.

The truest thing about my campaign: Make America Great Again. We will learn from this election. What I did will make America great again. We're changing the world, basically. No, I mean that: we're actually going to change the world.

Make America Great Again: make it educated again. You can't possibly get that angry if you know a little bit about anything.

Let me get serious: Ignorance cannot continue to be the cultural cornerstone of the United States of America. I've gotten rich — really rich — off a lot of others' ignorance. But you know what? I can't sit around and watch things get worse and worse forever. Besides, that's not good for business. There's a tipping point where it's not good anymore. When people are too stupid — I keep saying stupid. Uneducated. — to do what's in their own best interest, there's no negotiating with them, there's no motivating them. Business stops functioning. This is where we're headed.

This is why I stepped in and saved the country, so that my kids can have a business and I can have a dynasty. They weren't going to have anything if I didn't do this for Hillary and for the country. You can't operate a business empire in an overwhelmingly ignorant country. You can't get qualified people. The population votes against its own interest. The roads and bridges and rails crumble. The systems get hacked.

That's one thing we Clintons and Trumps have in common: we build dynasties. The Obamas have no imagination that way. They're so average. You think a black President is historic? No. A woman President. That's historic. Think about it: black countries had black presidents or kings or dictators long before they had woman presidents. History has resisted female leaders. And for good reason. It's a huge distraction, for one thing. And Hillary won't be the last. She won't be the last. Mark my words. Chelsea is on the way, and my children too. There *will* be a President Trump, but it won't be me. That's by choice.

I turned a million dollars into quote-unquote ten billion dollars, but here's the thing: that won't be my greatest achievement. I singlehandedly got a President in office who should've never had a chance. She was washed up. I know it; we all know it. Hill was so washed up…you know…look: we had to do something. When a cranky, geriatric socialist grandpa is gonna beat out the standard bearer of the party, you know that something was so wrong. If we hadn't started back in '08, it would've been game over. Game over for Hillary.

Chapter 1

What's Good for Business is Good for America

What's good for business is good for America. I mean really this was my campaign, right? I'm a good businessman, so I can run the country. We tested it out with Herman Cain: a successful career in business means a successful political leader (not politician; I'm not a politician).

It's ironic. It's such irony. Immigration is always good for business. Anybody knows that. And this is how far it's gone: when you have head of an international business empire campaigning against immigration, you have to know it's not real. You just have to know it. Look at what's in front of your nose. But this is where we are with education in this country: they can't tell a bowling ball from a powder brush when it hits them in the face.

Nothing the Republicans have been selling is good for business. Nothing. The only ones who think deregulation is good for business are the ones who can't cut deals. Without laws in place, you can't get a longterm advantage over the competition. It's a free-for-all. You might be on top one week, but they next week you go under. Look at 1989. I went from one of the richest guys in the world to having more debt personally – personally – than some small countries.

A Republican administration would be a horror story for my business. All they had to do was run a decent candidate. Scary moment: 2012. Jon Huntsman announces he's running. If he wins the nomination, we're screwed. Screwed. That's the end of Hillary. Four years of planning, Birther-ism, setting up 2016, all down the drain.

Republicans have been awful for business and for the economy. Bush and Bush both left recessions for Bill and Barak to clean up. Luckily, I learned from it the first time around. I respect the Bushes as politicians but they don't know what they're doing when in office. They don't know how to govern. It's cronyism at it's worst. You gotta have some competence running things.

I gotta tell you I was disappointed in Hillary for that. That was real disappointment. I had to attack her for something just to keep the game going. That was real. You don't put a donor on a top secret advisory board. It was a nice thing to attack her with, because nobody cares. You can't get too mad about a scandal if you can't even comprehend it. When you start saying Intelligence Advisory Board, you lose the public. Too much to explain. They can't handle it. It's just noise.

I stopped giving to Republicans because they're a bad investment. They doubled down on a shrinking population: white males. When you go into a new venture, you don't ask, what's the fastest shrinking population I can market this to? The only way a Republican wins in 2016 is with a moderate, independent nominee who picks up center-left voters and some minorities. The primary process makes that impossible.

2012 allowed us to test it out. When we got

Herman on top of the polls, we knew it could be done. As soon as we got Huntsman out, Hillary was in for 2016.

You can't be a party of nothing. If you say no to every deal, you never generate revenue. The Republicans needed someone who can get things done. I can get things done. Unlucky for them, they don't benefit. I did what I wanted. My family will make so much money in the next eight years, it will be unbelievable. Unbelievable. I'm telling you.

I'm not selfish about it. This is a win-win for me and the country. Hill is gonna get the job done, there's no question. She's prepared her whole life for it. Yeah, I'll benefit – my family will benefit – more than most. But everyone will benefit.

Look: the more you make and the more you're able to spend, the harder this train keeps charging. The great American economic engine. I don't know much about economics, but I know that. The voters don't know the difference between business and economics. They think what's good for business is good for the economy. It's the other way around. I can't help the economy. The economy helps me. That's the only way Hill has it better than me.

That's her leg up. It's not even a leg up, but it's something.

I bragged about creating thousands of jobs. The President creates millions of jobs. Millions. Or helps. Jobs mean spending. Spending means new deals, new projects.

We're gonna make Trump greater than ever and America greater than it's been in a long time. It's a win-win.

Chapter 2

All About

My 'Bill'-ions

Bill and Hill get me. They get what I do. And I get them. It works. It just works.

They want to be in charge, I mean in office. They love it. I don't know why they love it, but they love it. If you really want to be in charge, you gotta be in business. Everybody knows that. Business is power. I cut deals, I come out on top. Always.

There's nothing not to like about them. You do something for them, they do right back to you. And I have zero respect for the Republicans. Zero. You know why? They couldn't get the job done. I gave them a lot of money. A lot. Over many years. You know what I got in return? Zilch. Zero. Nothing. The Clintons are the best investment I could make. In the '90s, I went from billions in the red to billions in the black. That's really how Bill was the first black President. He put me in the black again.

Political campaigns are the cheapest and highest return you can get on your money. A few thousand turns into millions overnight. Bill and Hill and I have a great thing going. A great thing. Too good to let go and start over. Barak is fine. But the Obamas are average. They're average.

Look: anyone can make a family. You gotta be exceptional to make a dynasty, an empire. The Clintons have it right. They want three Presidents. I want a business empire. You can't be mushy gushy about family if you want greatness. It breeds mediocrity.

The greatest families have always been dynasties. Look at the Chinese. They've never been invaded in their history. A family is a business partnership. It's how America was built. Your kids are your labor, and you leave them the farm. For the Trumps, it's a business empire. The Trump name is only getting started. That's love. Handing your kids the world. That's love. Not hugs and kisses. Hugs and kisses are how people console themselves when they haven't accomplished anything. This is what the Clintons understand too. They get it.

If I want my adult children to do something, I pay them for it. They respect me because I can pay them. I'm not going to beg my children to do anything. I don't beg. There's a fine line between respect, fear and hate. We toe that line, and we win. We understand it and so do the Clintons. If your kid gets out of line, you threaten to disinherit. It's happened maybe a half a dozen times, and it works.

Family is an extension of the self. The broader the reach of your family, the more power you have. I want my daughters to be beautiful and my sons to be powerful. And they are. I'm sitting on top of the world. Literally. Trump Tower Presidential Suite. And I don't even have to do the job.

The weakest people do favors and get favors in return. Do yourself a favor: don't do favors. Don't do them. If something's important, you pay for it. Family or no family. If you have to beg your family for help, you've failed at life. I provide for my family. Immediate family, extended family. Friends. I'm the provider. I'm the man. That's why I financed my own campaign. Besides, anyone who knows anything knew I'd never be President, so why would they give? That's throwing money away. I'm not going to ask for money. I've never asked for money. Even when I lost everything, I fought my way back to the top. Nothing was a favor.

If you have to make people feel good to have friends, you're an emotional whore. Money is the great engine of friendship. That's why we use the word "value." I value you. If you have no money to back it up, you can't value someone.

The value of the Clintons for me is immeasurable. Who else can you give a few thousand dollars to every four years and get millions? Yeah, I send my friends their way too, but I'm only out a few thousand. It's basically free, and they love me for it. Bill and Hill and I have been at it for decades. Hill was always the plan. Barak threw a wrench in it, but we got over that. It wasn't the smoothest or easiest, but we got over it.

We had to do something extraordinary to make Hillary 2016 happen. Extraordinary. It wasn't going to happen on its own. There was nothing inevitable about 2016. '08 was supposed to be it.

When that didn't happen, it looked bad. Very bad.

You think Bill is the political mastermind? Let me tell you he's not. Bill is a smooth talker and he can sweet talk you, but he doesn't have the vision to get this done. Only I have the vision. It's my vision. He couldn't have come up with this. There was only one way to 2016, and I couldn't trust anyone else to handle it. I had to get myself into politics.

Bill actually paved the way for me. Want to run for President but have a playboy misogynist womanizing past? Let Bill and Monica pave the way. The public is totally desensitized. You can say "blowjob" on the nightly news, and they don't blink. Not to mention Anthony Weiner (also a friend of the Clintons). There's no way I could've run before '97.

Let me tell you something: if you want to be in politics, you don't tell the world how much money you have. Look at Loser Romney. One of the biggest losers I've ever met. They only good thing Romney ever did was teach me how to lose deliberately. Deliberately. Don't forget it. If I wanted to win, I would've won.

So I brag about my ten, eleven billion dollars. It's not $11 billion. Everybody knows that. I'm rich. Very rich. But you can't put a number on it. I have deals going in, falling out, going through, falling through all the time. It's the most fluid thing in the world. I don't have a net worth. I have constant financial motion, up and down. It's like the ocean. That's how I've been so successful. I'm not trying to hold on to anything. I'm always going for more. Is it risky? Absolutely. You gotta be willing to take the risks. Otherwise, you're not going anywhere.

I risked making a fool of myself to hand Hill the Presidency. You know why? It's worth it. I'll make deals like you wouldn't believe. You won't believe how successful the next eight years will be for me. And you know what? It's gonna be huge for Trump Hotel Washington D.C. I'm seen as a political figure now. I got more primary votes than any Republican in history. You can't get that kind of prestige on TV.

The prestige my campaign brings to Trump Hotel D.C. is beyond anything you can imagine for a hotel, and for the brand all around the world. And it's beautiful. You won't believe how beautiful it's gonna be. It's the most prestigious, most luxurious hotel that's ever been in that dumpy swamp of a city. I never stayed overnight in D.C. in my life. Never. Now I might go stay in my hotel. I might.

Chapter 3

Birth er' a Master Plan

Birtherism was so easy. So easy. You say something outrageous, you have a voice. The more outrageous the better. You've gotta have a voice and you gotta have power first. If there's one thing I have, it's a voice. I say it, the world hears. The more outlandish the better. That's how you make the news.

The things I said, I could've been on the street corner holding a cardboard sign. But when you have a few billion dollars behind what you say, people listen.

What do we know about Republican voters? White, ignorant, suppressed. The anger is boiling. They're the "against" party. Against minorities, against immigrants, against regulation, against equality, against the safety net, against government, against abortion. I have no idea how many women I've slept with have had abortions. Without abortion, I'd be a great grandfather already and I'd be the father too. When you bang that many 19-year-old women over that many years, one of them's bound to be your daughter if not for abortion. I love abortion. You want to ban something? Ban condoms. I'm so sick of women whining "use a condom, use a condom." If I wanted to screw a plastic sheet I'd let Goldie Hawn blow me. Believe me, she would. She wanted to before she was plastic. I wouldn't let her.

With Birther, I'm a hero. I called the President un-American, a non-American. I suggested he had a dark [no pun intended] agenda to basically dismantle the country. This stuff is irresistible to the media. Irresistible. It taps into the anger. It's perfect.

And it got me on the map politically. We found a legitimate way to say Barak didn't belong here. Southern white trash and rural midwesterners – they're the same thing – are feeling they just don't want a black man in office when I say he wasn't born here. It's code. It works. It's beautiful.

You look at GOP primary candidates trying to tap into the evangelicals. You can't. You can only get so far with the evangelicals when you're one of them. That's how I won them. I wasn't one of them. Nobody ever mistook me for a minister. They saw through Ted Cruz. What a joke. If there was ever a used car salesman running for President, it was Lyin' Ted. It's pandering. People don't want to be pandered to. They want a force of nature.

I saw it with W: he was a horrible President. Horrible. The worst President in history. Year 2000, after 8 years of Bill: world peace, budget surplus, economy and jobs growing, America respected around the world, Bin Laden on the run. Remember: it was the Republicans calling Bill "crazy" because he was "obsessed" with Bin Laden. Then W. came in, said forget about Bin Laden, slashed taxes for the rich, then the biggest government spending increase in history – a prescription drug payout to drug companies – got us attacked, got us into two wars, huge deficits, Great Recession, over 10% unemployment. Yet he was re-elected. Re. E-lected. I couldn't believe it. I didn't bet on it, but if I had, I would've lost.

When I started Birthering, I remembered what they did to John Kerry. Swiftboating. Same thing. Turned a war hero into Hanoi Jane. I don't know what was true. I just remember it worked. If that can get W. re-elected. It's unimaginable. You want to blame someone for me? Almost-President Trump? Blame Karl Rove. That man laid the groundwork. He's the reason we got Hill. Rove set up a house of cards that fell – a flash-in-the-pan, sure-to-die right wing electoral coalition. In it's place, we got House of Cards – Hill and Bill (aka Claire and Frank).

Chapter 4

O Say Cain You See

9-9-9. Are we dialing for pizza or voting for President? 9-9-9. Sheesh. First of all, it lost. When do you see me praising losers? When I marched Herman Cain out on stage with me, a man who closed a primary debate with the lyrics to the Pok-E-mon, you didn't know my candidacy was a sham? 9-9-9. 9-9-9!

This was the model. Cain was the model and the dry run. The Godfather of Pizza. Nobody would've ever known the name Herman Cain if I hadn't pushed him on stage. We had to test the waters in 2012. Republican voters would've voted for a naked sherpa wearing a duck floatie tube around his waist if he delivered his lines with strong enough conviction: that's how neglected they were for decades. They were like a Miss Universe runner-up the night the pageant ends: they would go home with anything measuring 98.6 degrees.

Jon Huntsman

Cain couldn't have happened in a vacuum. Actually, he had to happen in a vacuum: the complete absence of anything life-sustaining for the GOP. When they lost Hunstman, the only one who could've won "the general," they lost their last hope. The fact that Herman Cain far outpolled Jon Huntsman speaks volumes. The American voter – especially the GOP voter – has cornered the market on Stupid.

When Hunstman dropped out, that was the clincher for me. I knew I could take the primary in 2016. You had the best candidate beaten out in the primary by a bunch of nutjobs. The GOP was ripe for devastation, and I was the Grim Reaper. That's why we had to get rid of the Republican party. They were past the point of hope. They were weak. That's when you go in for the kill.

Speaking of polls, if you want no legitimacy whatsoever, base your campaign on your polling success. Because as soon as you're down, you've lost your legitimacy. You may think I'm dumb. But I'm not dumb enough to think I'd stay on top of the polls forever. But when I was on top, what did I do? I mentioned every poll out there. Every single poll. I'd go on and on about where we were in the polls. Nail in the coffin. I knew Hill would get ahead of me in the general polls. I laid the foundation for her legitimacy by using it as mine in the primary: he (or she) who tops the polls has legitimacy.

Think about it: why would I call Romney a loser and then appear with Herman Cain, praising him? Herman Cain is a huge loser compared to Romney! Cain didn't even win the primary. I try to let you in on my joke, but you suckers just don't get it. 9-9-9? Are we dialing in an emergency? Build a wall! 9-9-9! Racial profiling at our borders! I'm Hansel leaving a trail or breadcrumbs for you: all you have to do is follow the trail to the witch's house: my campaign is a sham! But you're so dense, to put it mildly, you're wandering clueless in the forest, gleefully stomping every crumby clue I drop.

George W. Bush

What Bush and Rove did was send the party off the deep end. They turned John McCain into a right wing nutjob. John McCain. If 1990s Independent, semi-principled McCain had run in 2008, he would've run away with the election. He would've been Bernie before Bernie was Bernie. Policy doesn't matter. Politics is personal. I say semi-principled. Does anyone else remember McCain was Mr. Term Limits? That didn't last long. Now he's Mr. Limitless Term. And how about Sarah Palin? If there was ever absurd enough a campaign to prepare the public for me, she was it! Thanks, Moose Lady! I learned a lot about how to talk to voters from Moose Lady. The woman can't form a sentence. She took W.'s speaking to a new level of dumb.

You listen to me on the campaign trail: "good" "bad" "great" "great" "great." The other day, I had the gall to say "she gets rich by making you poor." Talk about the pot calling the kettle black! Nobody noticed. Nobody. That's how I made my career. You couldn't make this stuff up. You couldn't.

I couldn't have spelled it out easier:

T-h-i-s i-s a j-o-k-e. Yet I was still basically neck-and-neck in some polls. Behind, deliberately, but very close. Only in a country where W. was re-elected – the worst President in history – re-elected. Only here could I poll in line with Hill. It's ignorance. Simple ignorance.

Chapter 5

A Left Crook and a Right Jeb

You can't run Hill against a moderate, clean Republican candidate. You just can't do it. Too much baggage. I knew this from the beginning. She's dirty, and everybody knows it. You have to be dirty to get things done. The nice guy doesn't win. Conventional wisdom said the Dems would hit 'em with a Left Crook [Hillary], and the GOP would hit back with a Right Jeb.

Neither one has any charisma. That's where I came in. Next to Jeb, I suck all the air out of the room. We've got me, Jeb, a bunch of far right nutjobs, a total loser failure at business [Fiorina, not to mention have you seen that face?] – that's a non-starter next to me. Another non-starter, Christie. Bridge construction, anyone? And Kasich, who has no recognition and no personality. After Jeb, if not me, it would've been Little Marco. He shot himself in the foot. Kasich would've been the next President if I'd have backed him, but why would I do that? He never did squat for me. Squat.

Jeb was so easy to take down. So easy. Next to me, he looks like a lady librarian. He's Barbara and Laura Bush combined in a man's body, except Barbara has more balls than he ever will. I'll say this: the voters can only be strung along for so many years. After thirty years of exploitation, it starts to unravel, and they didn't change up the playbook. Jeb was a copy of a copy [W.] of copy [H.W.] of Reagan. What works in 1980 doesn't work in 2016. If I were doing business the same way I did in 1980, I'd be out on the street.

Nobody had the gall to call a spade a spade on a political stage. Put me on a stage, I'll suck the air out of the room. You think a debate is anything compared to a negotiating table? You have hundreds of millions of dollars on the line, you have to perform. Politicians can't compete with a real showman.

If you're a real showman, you don't go into politics. Politicians are mostly bookworms and frat boys who've learned to jump through hoops. There's no creativity, nothing off-the-cuff. No agility on their toes. They're cardboard. Like Jeb. Just a prop to knock over.

Chapter 6

What Really Berns My Craw

I didn't need to win the primary. In a way, it makes things easier, but I lose another eight months of my life. Bernie cursed me with the nomination. It's a blessing and a curse, but we could've gotten the job done without it. I'm losing eight months of my life thanks to Bernie F. Sanders. You know what the F. is for. His parents didn't give him a middle name, so I just gave him one. You don't want Trump to name your kid? Do your job.

If Little Marco had pulled it off, which he should have – He shouldn't have tried to be me. That's what killed him. When he started talking about private parts, he was done – Then I could've jumped on the phone or on a TV interview once in awhile during the general. Now I'm on the trail for eight more months.

We have more control now, but I could be building hotels. I want to get going on these Moscow projects. I'm a hero over there now. They love me. Vladimir and are going to cash in like you wouldn't believe.

I hate delays. Hate 'em. You can imagine how mad I was at Barak and Ted Kennedy. Ted Kennedy betrayed me on that bigtime. Talk about Lyin' Ted. Forget Ted Cruz. Lyin' Ted Kennedy. I was a donor. A big donor. Then he backed Barak. That was not the deal.

Karma though. Sorry, Ted. You made me wait eight more years for Hillary. I made it work, but I didn't like it. Payback: I did better in the primary than you ever did. You will always be your brother's brother. I'll be *the* Trump. And now I've done the impossible and gotten my girl Hill where you always wanted to be. Not being President was the biggest failure of your life. You could've done it so many times. But you didn't know how to do good back to those who did good by you.

We tried to give it to Marco, but Bernie made that impossible and, ultimately, unnecessary. I don't like anything about Bernie. This is a loser, people. He had the nomination. He had it. Which would've pissed me off way more. But in the end, all I had to do was be him. Actually, he turned into me. The white-haired socialist me. Stubborn, loud, crotchety. No class. The no-class Trump. He's poor. Never succeeded in anything in his life. When he had influence for once in his life, he didn't know what to do with it.

Principles don't get you anywhere in life. Principles shoot you in the foot. Drag you down when you're on top. McCain knew he had to bail on his principles, he just did it at the wrong time and went the wrong way with it. W. was an exception, not the rule. McCain trying to be W. worked as well as Little Marco trying to be me.

Bernie can't understand how some voters were undecided between me and him. Loser mentality. When you're that out of touch with the real world, there's no helping you. Nobody cares about the issues. Nobody understands the issues. It's how strong and loud and independent and unwavering you are. That's how you appeal to the ignorant masses. When you ask them to understand things, you lose them.

Bernie's biggest mistake: thinking the issues were what made him. His strengths were his stubbornness and confidence and independence. When you're up there with a bunch of lifeless politicians – no soul. none. – all you have to do is show some life. Some vitality, virility. It's how you get women. Something Bernie wouldn't understand. I mean look at his wife.

He didn't see his own greatest strength. He fell into it by accident. When voters can't tell the difference between you, Bernie, real public servant, and a sham candidate, me, you're doing something really wrong. Really wrong.

Bernie would've been a terrible President. Terrible. Four years of ineffectual nothing. Nobody would benefit. He lives in a fantasy where the people are not totally clueless. His popularity is a fad, not a revolution. He has no friends in Washington. He's not one of them. Like Lyin' Ted but worse because he can't be bought.

My campaign is the revolution. Nobody has ever done this. It will actually make America great again, just not in the way they thought: not by building a wall, not by keeping Muslims out, by getting the people to awaken to their own ignorance. That was Socrates, right? I know my own ignorance. Nobody knows the name Socrates anymore. That's how ignorant we are.

Chapter 7

Making Hillary Great Again

I thought I could take a mainstream turn and still lose, but polls had us scared. Even the hint of mainstreaming gave me a bump! They wanted so badly to vote for me. Anyone but Hillary. It was hard work to out-"Anyone but" her. I had to make her the "Anyone but Trump," rather than myself the "Anyone but Hillary." I had to take a nosedive to Make Hillary Great Again.

She'll be a fine President. She just can't campaign. She doesn't connect. Politics is personal. She's not a person. But she's a governing machine. She gets it done. It's all for her, but she's done well for herself. I mean, the first woman rising to the top.

I gotta tell you, there aren't many women like her. She's not the type I go for personally, but it's a heck of a one-two punch, the Trumps and Clintons.

Private and public. Two sides of the coin. A big, fat, golden coin. I don't know what they do, but I know it works and I know I can count on them to line people up, and I line people up for them. Two-way street.

I've seen a lot of women. A lotta women. Believe me. These pageants. When you have money, women follow, okay? There aren't a lot like Hill.

Her chance was 2008. She had it. The same anti-establishment sentiment that propped me up put Obama on the board. And Hill had some enemies. You can't avoid it if you're going to accomplish anything. When you win, somebody else loses. The Clintons have been winning for a long time. Republicans try to immortalize Reagan, but it was Nixon who created the electorate for every Republican who has won. Bill did the same for Democrats. Gore almost won, he essentially won. Bush was an accident until 2004, when it was right back to 1972. I credit Bill with basically winning '92, '96, 2000, '08 and '12. Obama is Clinton 2.0. Hill is Clinton 3.0, or 1.0. They've always been a one-two punch. I'm telling you, House of Cards. Republicans have been putting themselves out trying to blow it down. They won't. They've run out of steam.

We had to make her great again. After 30 years of the GOP dragging her through the mud, the only way to do that was to make the other side so bad. So bad. That's where I stepped in.

Racism? Check. 1st grade vocabulary? Check. Empty, incoherent speeches? Check. Authoritarian tendencies? Check. Constant self-sabotage? Check. We tried to make her look like Joan of Arc – or something. Who is a good example? – while still running what looked like a campaign. But we didn't even really try to hide it. She's gonna be bigger than Joan of Arc. She'll be Cleopatra without the looks and the snakes.

What did I attack her on? Emails? Boring. Benghazi? Beaten to death. Crooked? Been digested and shat out a decade ago; no potency. Intelligence Advisory Board? The public can't even understand what it is.

Nobody else could've done this. I made Hillary great again. We made history. The first woman President. And I'm proud of her. She deserves it.

She and Bill have always had my respect, and we've always had each others backs. The public hasn't known it, but that's what makes it work.

The best alliances are always secret alliances. It's what won us WWII. It's how we got our first woman President. Well, I did, really. I did. And they say I'm a womanizer. I'm a woman-President-izer. I've done more for women than any woman ever did.

Chapter 8

Putin' the Smack Down

We couldn't just fall flat. It wouldn't do anything for Hill. If I died out single digit polling early in the primary, I wouldn't have changed the landscape enough to guarantee it for Hill. I had to put the smack down on the GOP field. I didn't have to win it. Let's make that clear: I never had to win the primary. I just had to be the Achilles heel of the GOP.

We had to tap into something. You've seen it in Europe the last fifteen years: right wing electoral strength. Neo-Nazism, xenophobia, anti-immigrant, Nationalism, anti-globalization. Le Pen, Hofer, Golden Dawn. Jobbik. Nobody had tapped into it yet here. Ripe for the picking. Nobody. One of two major political parties standing on the edge of a cliff, waiting to be pushed.

They were too afraid to cross the P.C. line. You can't be P.C. and tap into anger. That's why Santorum failed. Lipstick on a pig.

Putin is the master. I love Putin. Putin is fantastic. I admire him. I really do. We're gonna put a Trump Tower in Moscow. Trump and Putin standing tall in Russia. They crave class over there. We're gonna give it to them.

Putin, old-style authoritarian. That's the only thing W. and I agreed on. Putin and his friend Medvedev, placeholder proxy. Putin's return to power should've been our #1 worry. You can't stronghold an old empire that long without turning dangerous. He's John Wayne and Khrushchev rolled into one. The only thing holding Russia back from being a fascist state is the internet. You just can't get that kind of cult following on a mass scale anymore. But you can get somewhere in the ballpark.

Khrushchev. Now that's power. The greatest nation that ever graced the Earth, 1950s America, feared Khrushchev's Russia. And the Russians knew they were the other superpower. The average American today doesn't even feel like part of a superpower.

If you want to tap into anger, I'll tell you there's nothing like anti-semitism for that. I love Jews. My son-in-law is a Jew. Jew's are great. You can't be blatant about it. We didn't even notice the blue star. These hate groups have subtler codes we rely on. The star was less subtle. We should've caught that.

They acted in the media like it was some revelation that we got it from a white supremacist site. That's the strategy. That's our strategy. Use the material – most of it is under the radar. Use it on a level your average person, which means journalist, doesn't catch on to. The mainstream media won't run a conspiracy theory, because we won't give them access. And that wasn't even the Washington Post. You give them too much credit. They weren't onto anything. They're just bad at their jobs. It's TMZ. The Washington Post is the new TMZ.

We take the language and posts that aren't obvious. The subtle ones. We post those. Then if the internet goes crazy about how we got it from a site, that's more coverage. And we get the most loyal supporters from the white trash. It's beautiful. It's great.

Never admit you're wrong. Never. It's weakness.

You lose all credibility. I've never admitted I was wrong, and I never will. You can't be wrong and have respect. Hill said she was wrong about gay marriage. I keep telling her she can't play it so safe and slippery. Makes her look Crooked. She'll never change at this point. Old dog.

Gay marriage is done as a political issue. It's done. 2004 was the last time that worked. Putin can do it over there. Russia is still in the Middle Ages in a lot of ways. I know. I've been there. Putin plays the gay card and it works. Elton is trying to do something about that. It won't work. I can't publicly be for gay marriage. I use the language on Supreme Court nominees to run a campaign. It's so backward. We're handing it to Hillary. If I were for gay marriage, I would've won.

Clarence Thomas was at Rush's wedding when Elton was there. He will never vote for a gay issue, but he has nothing against gays either. Elton is his favorite too. His basement man cave is all Elton vinyl. We all love Elton. He would've played at my inauguration.

People complained about Elton playing at Rush's wedding. You have to understand, it's all an act. Rush's radio mentor was gay. He died of AIDS with Rush holding his hand to the last breath in the hospital. Rush has nothing against gays. Neither do I. It's business. Elton understands that; he doesn't like it, but he understands it. He wants it to change. But being backward will always be a way to get a lot of support. Maybe not the majority, but a lot. Enough to make a killing on the radio.

I gotta tell you, when a bunch of gays getting taken out – and I don't care if they're gay – let's just say a bunch of 20- / 30-something men, gay or not. When a bunch of men get taken out in a seedy bar and that gets more done on gun control than a school full of kindergarteners, the world has changed. Society values the individual more than the family. That's all it is. The people can sympathize more with adult victims, and the gay part just makes them more independent. The independent adult is celebrated more than the family.

I couldn't have run 30 years ago because nobody would honestly call me a family man. But boy am I independent. That's why they love me. The family part is enough to tell them I'm not a nutjob. If I were a single man saying what I do... But I have a beautiful wife, successful grown children and a beautiful son. It's great. They make me look like an old world king. They prop me up, I give them a dynasty. It's great.

Obama's immigration plans, especially being a foreigner himself (ha!), made the choice of proposals easy for my team. Scapegoating immigrants won't get you a win, but it will get you on the map. Especially with out-of-work and underemployed, uneducated voters being left behind for so long. They got nothing in return for their votes for 30 years. Nothing. Couldn't go on forever. The GOP took them for granted. When you make a deal, you have to deliver or you have to get out. They were playing Atlantic City with poor white voters but they never cashed out and moved to the next mark. They stayed in town and went down with the ship.

Chapter 9

Systematically Dismantling the GOP

It's not that I disagree with their policies, although I really do. I just have no respect for these people. It's no way to run an organization to let people who know nothing about your business choose your C.E.O. It would be like letting the shareholders of a publicly traded company nominate their own candidates and then elect the C.E.O. from them. You'd end up with Vin Diesel running Tesla Motors. That was W.

You've got a coke-snorting, C- student who failed at school, failed at business and knew zero about running a country. Zero. I know almost nothing. He knew nothing. The difference between me and W. is I know I couldn't run the country. I'm brash but

I'm not dumb. I went to Wharton. You can't scrap all our treaties and expect to negotiate new ones. There'd be no expectation of follow through. If we just bail on the agreements we have, there's no confidence in our word. I know that. How my voters didn't see that, well. That's the whole point.

The GOP got complacent. They're the alternative to the Democrats. They haven't had an agenda for decades. Who runs a business to put itself out of business? Less government, when you're the government? What kind of a plan is that? De-regulate when it's your job to regulate? Did they miss that part of the Constitution? They claim to be the Constitutional experts.

When the poor and middle class see no gains in income, you lose their allegiance. The Democrats have a model to go from. The Republicans are looking backward: Reagan, the Constitution, the Bible. These things don't apply in today's world. It's a worthless party. The extent to which it was a vacuum is obvious given my success. I had no connection to the GOP. None. But I took it over. It wasn't even hard. I took it over in 5 months. That's how weak and rudderless it was. Now I've decimated it. It's the greatest political achievement in our history.

Chapter 10

Mindful

Mindlessness

Look at MJ. Not Jordan. Michael Jackson. Forget the rumors and tabloids. As a dancer. As a dancer. Fred Astaire, James Brown led to Michael. I love Michael. I knew him. You didn't know him. I did. He took Fred Astaire and James Brown and others and put his stamp on it and made it his own. He was the greatest entertainer. The greatest.

I took W. and Palin and Cain and took it up two notches. Nobody can deny I tapped into something. What I tapped into was ignorance. Pure, unadulterated ignorance. The anger. The racism. When you're going through life blind, it's scary. It's dark. It's scary. You want a firm hand to guide you. It doesn't matter where, as long as the hand is firm and steady. Elections are pure emotion. There's no rational thought that goes into a vote.

I said as little as possible as strongly as possible. Simple declarative sentence. Good, great, fantastic, awesome. I love you. "I love the poorly educated." Hellooooo? Hellooooo? Anyone listening? I love the poorly educated! I watched them support W. I watched them support Palin. Cain. Me. It's all I needed to fan the flames of the GOP circus.

It worked. That's it. It worked.

I succeeded by being deliberately mindless. Almost half our population is mindless, ignorant, uneducated, or, what was it, Mitt? 47 percent? You look strong, rich, stubborn, steady; it doesn't matter what you say. They get behind you.

They want a father figure, or these days a grandfather figure. Why are candidates getting older and older? [Again, Barak was the exception.] I'm too old to be President, so is Hill. Age comes with problems. You don't want the President dealing with age. I'm one of the healthiest 70 year olds on the planet. You still don't want me. It's a distraction.

We're all in our 60s and 70s. The generations are getting dumber. People know it. So you go with an old fart, hoping we are somehow better prepared than you.

I ran a sham candidacy and tried to lose and still got almost half of America to vote for me. It's ignorance. You think Zika is bad? Ebola? HIV? Ignorance is the epidemic. When my story gets out, people will wake up.

You've got a computer in your pocket at all times, a glowing screen in your face. It's a supercomputer. It's faster than the big towers that used to sit on our desks in the 90s. You have a supercomputer in your pocket. Isn't that what Jobs said? You have the whole world of information on it, and what to people do? They play arcade games. They scroll through photos. They watch cat videos. They take "selfies."

Maybe when they realize they voted for a joke, they'll look up a fact or two once in awhile. You can get a Harvard education on your phone. I'm not talking about the Iraq ISIS Harvard either. I'm talking actual Harvard. You can learn a language, research a candidate. When are the games and photos and funny cats going to stop? Do you need to elect a dictator first to wake up? A generation is being lost in its phone.

What a powerful tool. America, this generation all over the world, could be the most capable, powerful generation ever. Instead, they're watching cat videos and taking selfies. Did you see Wall-E? Barron and I watched it. This is where we are. Those screens are your phones. I'm your wake-up call, what Hill and I did. She's gonna be a great President. Win-win. But don't ever vote for a Trump again, America. If I ran for real, I'd be President. But the way I ran, I shouldn't have gotten a single vote. Not one. Wake up.

Chapter 11

If I Had Won

TRUMP: NATIONAL UNITY IS "SILVER LINING" TO MASS SUICIDES ON INAUGURATION DAY

WASHINGTON D.C. - January 21, 2017 - Today, President Donald Trump, in his first official White House press briefing, expressed in prepared remarks his hope that yesterday's mass suicides, now estimated at upwards of 46 million Americans, would result in "unprecedented national unity" that would "allow America to move forward with our bold agenda, unimpeded by the paralyzing epidemic of dissent and wrangling seen over the last eight years." He added, "We have total agreement now. Total agreement. You won't believe how much we're gonna get done. It's gonna be unbelievable."

While he offered condolences to surviving friends and families of the millions of departed, the

President offered off-the-cuff that "most of us who remain have always been on the same side of the fence, if you know what I mean; there wasn't much co-mingling going on" and that he "didn't personally know any of the people who took their own lives yesterday."

In his first statement on fiscal policy as President, Trump noted that "our goal of balancing the budget will be advanced by significant savings on Secret Service protection for the late Presidents Obama and Carter, as well as former Vice-President Al Gore, all of whom took part in yesterday's...ahem...event." Trump said there will be a discussion of whether to continue protection for President Clinton, who, according to a White House aide speaking on condition of anonymity, "is too much of a selfish, self-aggrandizing prick to go in peace with his colleagues."

When asked whether the new administration's agenda for its first 100 days included any initiatives on social issues, Trump replied, "the latest information on yesterday's shift in demographics suggests that gay marriage, immigration, racial profiling and affirmative action are "pretty much moot points now." He added, "We're going to save Mexico billions on the wall. Don't need it anymore. There aren't any Mexican Americans or immigrants left here. They think US soil is cursed now and the few who remain are running South. It's beautiful. I told you I'd solve immigration. I didn't expect to solve it this way, but a solution is a solution."

As for how the suicides would affect the economy in the coming years, Trump said, "I've already heard some very good ideas – great ideas, actually – for how the sudden boon of useable biomass can be utilized to achieve full energy-independence in the near-term" and that "the most enterprising Americans remain with us and will now be unimpeded by self-proclaimed 'stewards' who have so long obstructed the best plans out there for capitalizing on our national resources."

Trump closed his prepared remarks by noting that "we have yet to hear of any homicides among the millions of deaths yesterday, showing that America's perfect two-hundred-forty-year record of peaceful, democratic transitions of power remains untarnished."

www.ingramcontent.com/pod-product-compliance
Lightning Source LLC
Chambersburg PA
CBHW071237280526
45787CB00002B/969